Leading and Growing Small Manufacturing Businesses

A Personal Journey

Ibrahim Ibrahim

Foreword by Bob Emiliani

Leading and Growing Small Manufacturing Businesses / Ibrahim Ibrahim

Cover art by Alexia Dulieu

ISBN-13: 979-8-9936307-0-0
Library of Congress Control Number: 2025923276

1. Small Business 2. Manufacturing 3. Leadership
4. Management 5. Human Resources

First Edition: December 2025

Published by Lynn Welding, Newington, Connecticut

For my family Aya, Haya, and Maya,
Jan and Darius Kania, and
the people whose dedicated work
helps small businesses grow and prosper.
Together we succeed.

I also want to thank Professor Emiliani for helping, inspiring, and supporting me in writing this book. He has been a huge mentor throughout my career and has helped many of our employees who seek leadership coaching.

CONTENTS

Foreword

The proudest achievement of a professor, the academic programs they create, and the department they teach in is to witness the success of our former students. In nearly all cases our undergraduate and graduate programs have moved people forward in their careers, some to levels they never dreamed of. They don't just do well in school; they do well in their work and in life. That tells us that our programs, with their up-to-date content and practical orientation, serve students well after graduation. Their success in business is also surely the result of their own intelligence and hard work.

Ibrahim was a student of mine. He did well in the courses that I and others taught, turning in assignments on time and with high quality every time. I have worked with him since he graduated. It has been amazing to watch his growth over the last 12 years! From resistance welding process engineer to the Chief Operating Officer of Lynn Welding, while co-owning two related companies. All with his ever-present smile. It is a testament to the range of Ibrahim's vision, capabilities, intellect, relationship building, and drive to get important things done quickly. On behalf of my faculty team, we are all so proud of Ibrahim for what he has accomplished and what is yet to come!

Dr. Bob Emiliani
Professor Emeritus
Central Connecticut State University

Ibrahim and Bob Emiliani

Preface

It has been just 12 years since I graduated from college. During that time, I have devoted myself to improving the small aerospace business that employs me. It began with my work as a resistance welding process engineer, then department manager, operations manager, and now chief operating officer of the company.

I wanted to improve all aspects of the business, from human resources to sales and marketing, quality, technical capabilities, customer service, purchasing, accounting, information technology, and so on. I also wanted to improve myself – my capabilities for improving a business because I had an eye towards someday owning my own businesses. Doing this required building not just my technical and business capabilities, but building relationships to gain the trust and respect of others.

I was able to do this by first understanding the existing processes, then collaboratively identifying the problems and their causes and implementing solutions. If the solution did not work, we kept trying. We would quickly iterate to dig further into the causes of the problem and identify new solutions to implement. And we did this iterative improvement work quickly. Being a small business, we did not have to fight bureaucracy to get things done. The owner trusted me.

The owners could see that I was fully committed to

their business and working hard every day, often nights and weekends, to make it better, as if I owned the company. Not making the business better in a random way, but by always thinking about cause and effect.

The trust that the owner had in me led to us becoming business partners in two other businesses: an aerospace and defense business specializing in waterjet cutting and an aerospace and defense business specializing in resistance spot and seam welding.

Of course, this was not all just my doing. The dedicated managers and employees in each company have had very strong hands in helping to build better businesses. And I see more such opportunities on the horizon.

I believe that my experience is somewhat unique and that others small business leaders might want to learn my way of thinking about building better businesses and creating new businesses. This book will appeal to manufacturing entrepreneurs, which this country desperately needs more of, and owners of small manufacturing businesses.

I hope you enjoy this book and find it helpful in your never-ending quest to better serve your ever more demanding customers and build a better business.

Ibrahim Ibrahim
Newington, Connecticut
25 November 2025

Lynn Welding team in June 2011. Photo includes Jan Kania (owner), his son Darius, and Ibrahim.

Prologue

How One More Try Saved My American Dream!

My name is Ibrahim Ibrahim. When I was in high school, I wanted to go to Germany and learn engineering. My parents said, "Why don't you go to the United States? Your cousin lives there." I said okay. My visa process to the U.S. took five months, I finally got my access visa with eight days left and I received it two days late. So, I had just six days to fly from Egypt to the U.S. or my visa will be cancelled. I booked the flight and got ready in two days.

I landed at JFK airport in Queens, New York, on 11 March 2010 with $6,400 in my pocket. My visa was set to expire in two days. The Customs and Border Protection (CBP) Officer found that my paperwork from school expired because my visa was delayed five months, which is over the 90-day limit. The CBP officer said you will have to return to your home country and wait for the school, Central Connecticut State University (CCSU), to send you updated documents. That means I would have to apply for new visa. I said, "Can you please call the school?" He said, "It's 4:30 p.m. Everyone's probably gone home." I said, "Just try to call this number" number using the Google Translate app.

He called the immigration office at CCSU. The phone

kept ringing, and he said there was no answer. Using Google Translate I said, "Please try again." Later, I was told by the director of CCSU's International Student and Scholar Services (ISSS), Toyin Ayeni, that a staff member was locking her office and heard phone ringing and ringing. She decided to unlock the door and answer the phone. When she answered, the CBP officer explained the situation and she said, "Do not deport him!" She faxed the CBP officer temporary documents that allowed me to enter the U.S. until they renewed my I-20 form (foreign student residency). The lesson here is keep trying until the very last second, don't just cry and walk away. This is always my mindset. I am forever grateful for the extra effort made by the CPB officer and the staff member at CCSU's ISSS office.

I was picked up by my cousin and went to live in an apartment in West Haven, Connecticut, with a Moroccan guy, Adil, who was very kind. I was confused, insecure and lonely. I said it is okay, tomorrow will be better. It's only first day in America. I went to CCSU on the second day. I was accepted and joined the Intensive English Language Program at school. My cousin helped me find a room in a shared house near CCSU in New Britain, Connecticut. The house was owned by guy who had four female renters and me. I said it's okay; it's better than living in West Haven where I don't have a car. But who cares, I have a room.

I had no car and no phone for weeks. I was walking miles to everything, in cold snowy weather. But I said it's okay, things will be better. My cousin got me a phone and my cash was running very low after paying tuition. I asked for a job. He said, "You don't speak English. You must learn English first." So, I practiced English for 10 to 12 hours a day. I kept on asking for work to pay my rent. My cousin helped me buy a 1995 Toyota Camry for $1200 and that was my very last draw of cash.

I started to help him at his pizza shop as a driver. The shop was an hour away from where I lived, but at least I had some income. Working at his pizza shop was payback for him helping me pay for rent and living expenses. Between school, work, and commuting, it was a very busy time.

I passed the Test of English as a Foreign Language (TOEFL) and was accepted as a full-time student in the School of Engineering and Technology. That was my first success milestone. Two days later, I got a letter from CCSU's finance office that said I need to provide evidence that I can pay tuition as a foreign student and housing. My cousin did not have enough cash in his bank account to sponsor me. My parents paid for my tuition so I could focus on engineering while I worked to pay for my living expenses. The finance office said they do not accept bank statements from foreign banks unless they are certified.

So, I got the bank statements, got them translated and certified, and was then granted five years on my I-20 to stay in the United States to complete my education.

My first semester at CCSU was rough. I barely passed; my GPA was in the 2s. I used to sit in class completely lost. My English wasn't very good at all, and I often missed assignments or came unprepared simply because I didn't fully understand what was being asked. I still remember and will always be grateful to my professors who patiently tried to help me understand.

While I was working in my first semester at CCSU, the first thing I thought about was that I needed to find a job in engineering. My English was still weak, and I didn't know where to start. I went to the Career Development Office at CCSU, and they helped me write a resume and cover letter. I applied everywhere but had no luck. I mailed my resume to over 200 companies across the United States and got some interviews but had no luck getting a job because I was a foreign student. Most companies want someone who is authorized as a permanent resident in the U.S.

I found an advertisement for Lynn Welding on CCSU's internship website. It was an unpaid internship. I applied and on Friday I got a call from Darius Kania for an interview. It went very well. I saw potential in this company. Darius said the company was recovering from the 2008-2009 recession and he is helping his dad recover. Despite being an unpaid internship, I was excited because I finally got an opportunity. I was up against the wall. So, I worked there like there was no tomorrow to prove myself. After a few months, Lynn Welding started paying me. I quietly worked hard because I had no knowledge of business or of manufacturing. I was just learning as much as I could and trying hard to do good work.

In March 2012, I was close to graduation, and so I went to talk with Jan (Darius's father) and Darius about the possibility of working at Lynn Welding full time after graduation. I needed an employer to sponsor me as a skilled permanent U.S. resident to be able to stay in the United States. Darius was very welcoming and supportive, and I met with him during my graduation ceremony. He said, "See you Monday." Jan and Darius were always supportive and believed in me, which was a huge part of my growth and an important lesson in how to trust people and build teams. Jan would always tell me, "Don't worry. If you need something we are here for you." He and Darius always treated me with kindness and respect, and they trusted me. That played a huge part in my growth.

Since my internship days, it was very exciting going to work every day at Lynn Welding. I was always excited about my projects and thinking about how to make business better. I never asked for a raise, never had problems with anyone, always focused on my growth and what's best for the company. I started taking on really difficult tasks and doing the best I could to fix problems with a smile. I always had the mindset that if someone else was able to do it, we can do it too.

In early 2013, I got my first salary from Lynn Welding and a substantial raise and bought my very first brand new car. In September 2013, I bought a small beat-up house in Portland, Connecticut and fixed it up on my personal time. Years later I got my Permanent Resident card and then became a naturalized U.S. citizen in 2021.

In 2016, I was named the Operations Manager of Lynn Welding, after 5 years of rotating in every corner of the business with major growth. I continued to work hard, kept humble, never got comfortable.

In 2019, Darius and I started a new company, Intelligent Cutting Solutions (ICS). We opened our doors in August 2020 during the COVID-19 pandemic. We had virtually no business for six months but we decided to keep going. Today, ICS is one of the largest waterjet cutting companies in Connecticut. In 2024, Darius and I acquired Associated Spot Welders (ASW) in City of Industry, California, and quickly developed it to become a world class aerospace welding service on the west coast.

In 2025, I was named Chief Operating Officer of Lynn

Welding.

Going back to where I started at Lynn Welding, if I rejected unpaid internship, I wouldn't work here today and none of this could have happened. If I was complaining or doing a lousy job, the company would not have sponsored me to become a permanent resident, and I would have had to leave the U.S. after graduation.

If I was not growth oriented, taking on difficult challenges, and seeing the bigger picture, I wouldn't grow with the company and I wouldn't have made good money or been in leadership positions.

The lesson here is you must continue to work hard. Don't get comfortable, don't think you are better than anyone else, and don't limit your potential because if you stop growing, you are going backward. Love what you do until you do what you love, work with what you have until you get what you want. Be flexible, hustle, and adapt because nothing will be permanent. Change and keep moving forward with a smile.

Working a trade show, circa 2013.

Introduction

The purpose of this book is to share what I have learned with other small manufacturing business leaders. It includes a philosophy of business and matters related to operations, finance, and building relationships with team members, customers, and suppliers.

The foundation is to respect people in a deep way, not as a cliché. While various machine-based technologies can do a lot, it is people who do the work that will make the company successful. If people are not respected, not understood, then neither the company nor its people will rise to their potential. Leaders must carefully observe what is happening and listen to people – employees, customers, suppliers – in a non-blaming, non-judgmental way.

Leaders must listen more than they talk. Some do this well, but then nothing happens. What they hear are complaints, and the usual response is to ignore them. This destroys trust. Instead, leaders must act on what they have learned from listening to people. And leaders must keep people updated when they promise to do something. If you say, "I'll get back to you," then do it. If you forget to get back to them, they will think you are unreliable, disorganized, and inconsiderate.

With so much going on every day, leaders' minds are

easily overwhelmed and easily distracted. This loss of focus impairs thinking and decision-making. Business requires a lot of "doing," a lot of action to get things done. But too often the drive to do things overwhelms the need for thinking.

Leadership is improved when leaders learn to quiet their minds and become calmer in the face of daily challenges. Doing so is essential for leaders to develop their mental potential and be mentally present for the people who depend on us for help and direction. Leaders are in a position of authority, and so they must strive to be accurate in their thinking and decision-making. If so, people trust your guidance and decisions.

Accuracy in thinking and decision-making means going to the shop and office floor, speaking to people, and observing what is happening with a calm and quiet mind. In doing that, the leader will often be the mediator in conflicts between people or departments or conflicting views of the causes or severity of a problem. Sometimes you must play referee. But that role is effective only if the leader carefully listens to both sides of the story. Always trust the people but verify when necessary.

To avoid becoming a full-time mediator, the leader must be a team builder and teach people basic structured problem-solving methods. If this is not done, conflicts will be ever-present, and people will depend on the leader to solve all their problems. Instead, develop people's skills for autonomous problem solving so that the leader gets involved only for larger or more difficult problems.

Small manufacturing business leaders take pride in the products they produce. But the company is more than just products for customers. It is people too. Leaders must do the kinds of things that develop and grow team members' technical and interpersonal skills and capabilities. Have a positive impact on their lives and take pride in seeing your team grow as the company grows.

There is always pull towards arrogance that makes leaders think they know it all. This is a trap to avoid because it destroys trust and ruins teamwork. The leader must be conscious of the importance of being humble and open to learning from others no matter what their level of experience is. Every situation, no matter how obviously simple, offers opportunities to learn something new or to reflect upon. The imperious company leader is always disliked by employees and is therefore much less effective than they could be.

Small business leaders are busy people. They wear many hats and as a result may be impatient or short-tempered. They may get angry when problems arise and blame people for problems. Anger will make solving the problem more difficult and less effective.

Blaming people for problems instills fear in the workplace. Fear causes employees to hide problems, which means problems grow and become bigger. When those problems finally emerge, the leader again blames people. It is difficult to do, but the better way is to approach problems with kindness because nobody comes to work with the intent of creating problems and hope the boss will blame them.

As all small business owners know, business is one problem after another, every day, for as long as the company exists. Given that problems are ever-present in every business process, there is a great temptation to avoid problems and work on other things that are better aligned with the leader's interests or skills. This is a recipe for growing problems, not eliminating problems. It is better to face problems the moment they arise and solve them one-by-one instead of avoiding them.

Leaders cannot afford to drown in problems; they must delegate when needed, always being sure to keep high-level problems on your radar screen. The problem recognition and problem-solving capabilities of the leader must become expert level, and other leaders and team members should be upskilled in both.

I have found that in my journey it has been essential to make written notes of conversations about problems, ideas for solutions, and reflection. This helps define paths of action for improvement with an eye towards eliminating repetitive problems by creating systems and standards – both of which are not set in stone but subject to continuous improvement. Small businesses must establish systems and standards for all processes because they do not have the time or resources that large companies have. The leader has more time to lead and train team members when systems and standards are put into place – and quickly changed when needs change or when people have ideas for improvement.

All small manufacturing business leaders work hard. But often working hard means working ineffectively. I am sure many leaders sense that and would like to do better. But it is not possible to do better unless the leader devises a simple plan to do better, sticks to it, and believes in themselves. A big part of such plans is improving employee engagement so that some of the burden of management is lifted from the shoulders of the leaders. Higher levels of employee engagement make the business run better and help it grow faster. It is in the leader's interest to lead better.

These introductory comments share some of my philosophy of business and building relationships. Subsequent chapters will describe more of this, as well as matters related to operations, finance, and other aspects of leading and growing small businesses. Hopefully, this book offers small business leaders some useful guidance to create simple plans that help them become more effective leaders and team builders to grow their business.

1
Creating Company Culture

It is obvious to say that a company should be customer centric. After all, the customer is the source of cash that sustains a company's existence. But too often the customer is taken for granted by the management team. And when the management team takes customers for granted, so does everyone else in the company, including the employees who produce the products and services that customers buy.

It is also obvious to say management should respect people. Not just employees, but suppliers, customers, investors, the community, and even competitors. Too often employees are not respected by the management team. They are hired to do a job, they do it, maybe get a little feedback now and then – often negative in orientation – and that's it. When the management team does not respect employees, no matter their role, then people do not respect one another. This has a negative impact on all work processes in terms of teamwork, timeliness, and quality. And these, of course, affect customers and the ability of the company to grow and prosper.

The point of customer centricity and respecting people is to illustrate the interconnectedness of people, the work (processes), and outcomes. If the management team does not recognize the interconnectedness, then all they see is tasks that employees do day in and day out. The company culture that they unknowingly create is a culture where people are disconnected from the customer and do not work well together. The business may be successful from the standpoint of earning a profit, but it is nothing more than a company that gets the job done. That's good, and the owner can be proud, but does not build anything more substantial.

Company culture can emerge from the way the top leaders think and do things. Oftentimes, the way they think and do things is inconsistent and haphazard and thus lacks any organizing principles. Employees may tolerate working in such an environment, but it will not result in the type of culture that fully buys into the company's goals and consistently performs at a high level.

Company culture should instead be developed with intentionality in relation to the top leader's desired employee, customer, and business outcomes. What do you want to happen? What are the desired outcomes, specifically? Does the leader have vague ideas or concrete ideas? Is it happy employees, happy customers, 25 percent net profit margin and 5 percent compound annual growth rate? Or is it more basic; employees have jobs, customers get their orders, 10 percent net profit margin and 2 percent compound annual growth rate?

The leader's desired employee, customer, and business outcomes will be based on the leader's principles for managing people, processes, customers, and suppliers. The question is, what are the leaders' principles? Does the leader even know what they are? If not, a culture will emerge, which could be good or bad, thus leaving culture to chance rather than being built with intention.

The leader must give a lot of thought to the principles that will lead to the desired people, customer, and business outcomes. The principles, once established, will evolve over time, while some new ones may be added and a few may fade away as the culture takes shape and as circumstances change. The point is that the top leader must build the company's culture with intentionality based on principles that everyone in the company can understand and can rely on. This will result in better and faster decision-making at all levels.

All of this can sound easy to do, but it is not. It is a challenge to figure out desired employee, customer, and business outcomes and the related principles. And then, the leader must consistently and forever train employees in the desired employee, customer, and business outcomes and the related principles, and model the behaviors that support them. If the leader can do that, then their job, and everyone else's job, becomes easier.

It is easy to make things complicated, so instead strive

for simplicity in figuring out the desired employee, customer, and business outcomes and the related principles.

Below are several examples of principles for small manufacturing business leaders to live by. The leadership team should work daily to train employees to accept and value these company principles:

- Cohesive team mentality
- Cross training
- Customer service
- Can-do attitude
- Communication
- Active listening
- Share ideas
- Generate new ideas to try
- Creatively solve problems
- Attention to detail
- Quality work
- Efficiency
- Fairness
- Honesty
- Respectful of one another
- Safe and clean workplace
- Stable work environment
- Ethical responsibilities
- Punctuality

- Reliability
- Generous pay, bonuses, and benefits
- Empower employees to solve problems and make decisions
- Growth oriented
- Collaborate with suppliers to produce mutually beneficial outcomes
- Redundancy of critical equipment

Most of these principles should be made explicit for all employees to work by, while a few may be closely held by the leader.

Manufacturing is a fun business to be in because it is fast-paced and there are always interesting new challenges. The work we do is tangible in its rewards. There is great satisfaction in figuring out how to make the customer's product and the daily challenge of quickly solving many different kinds of problems. The daily delivery of products to customers gives the work meaning and instills is with pride in our work. If, as a leader, you see manufacturing as a fun business to be in, others will see it that way as well. This will help strengthen the team mentality that is essential for growing the business.

Helping to get the job done.

2
Guidance for Leaders

Leading a small business is more than making daily decisions. It is about building a culture of trust, consistency, and mutual respect while maintaining a focus on growth, profitability, and long-term sustainability. Here is what has worked for me, to help guide your leadership and business journey.

1. Use Data as Your Compass
Data is one of the most powerful tools available to small business owners. It turns guesswork into insight and enables sound decision-making. For example, if your accounting software like QuickBooks isn't updated daily, you might look at your profit and loss and think you're in a good place financially – only to later discover major cash flow issues when it's too late. Always keep your financials current.

Collections are the lifeblood of your cash flow. Winning sales is meaningless if you're not collecting. No cash flow means your operations are paralyzed. Make sure customer payments are timely, especially when you deliver on time. It must be a win-win.

I have a golden rule that your incoming accounts receivable must be higher than your accounts payable including payroll. If you are not on top of your collections, you will be forced to dip into your line of credit until your customers pay you. Now, what if your customers decide not to pay you due to a major event such as 9/11 or war or recession? Now you have a huge accounts receivable that is uncollectable and a huge debt that you must pay.

2. Trust, But Always Verify

Even if you deeply trust a team member, always verify the information they bring to you. Why? Because people's evaluation of situations varies based on emotions, experience, or biases. Someone may overreact and say there's a "disaster" when it's not. Another may downplay something that is, in fact, a serious threat to your business. As a leader, it's your responsibility to gather facts before acting.

Oftentimes, people walk to my office and say, "Everyone is upset about so and so." The question I ask is "Who is everyone? 1, 2, 5, or 10 people? Is it a specific department or the whole company? Based on that information, I react accordingly. It could be 2 people out of 100 employees, which is 2 percent of the workforce, and we can just work together to find a middle ground with them. It is not a disaster compared to 60 people who are upset, and we need to re-consider a decision.

You must also train your future leaders to recognize this. Help them learn how to assess risk, understand consequences, and make decisions based on reality – not emotion.

3. Lead Without Ego

You can't afford to lead with ego or emotions. If you're angry or upset, don't make decisions. Your mental state will impair your judgment no matter how experienced you are. Calm down, reset, and then act. Your ultimate goal is to achieve the company's vision. There are countless ways to achieve the goal. Choose the right approach for the right place and at the right time.

Sometimes people approach me and I can't tell if they are testing me or if they have a big ego. So, I don't immediately react if I start getting upset with what I am hearing. I usually say, "Okay. I don't really like that, but let's sleep on it. I want you to re-consider this and I will think about what you told me. Let's get together tomorrow." In doing this, I am letting the person temper their ego while I am defusing my own ego. The next day the person sometimes says, "I thought about it, and you are right, I was not reasonable," and we hash it out.

Or if they come in and they insist they are right, I can then explain "Well we can't offer you such and such, but here is what I can offer you if you want to work things out." We take it from there to hopefully find a middle ground.

I try to avoid showing anger or immediately saying "NO!" without thinking because I remember that I am human and I have emotions that I might not be able to control. But I can control how to suppress my emotion when it is not appropriate to react immediately. This requires a lot of training and self-discipline, but almost always results in better outcomes for everyone.

4. Leadership Is About Approach
Consider the difference between these two approaches:

Boss: "Hey, I need you to stay late and finish this job ASAP. I don't care how, just get it done."
Leader: "Hey, we need your help. Boeing is urgently pressuring us to complete this job. I know your wife is working and you have two kids. If you can't, I understand. But if you can help, even just today and Friday, I'd really appreciate it."

People are more likely to help when they feel respected, valued, and seen. Leadership is about purposefully building loyalty, not demanding obedience.

5. Build Personal Connections (With Boundaries)
Your team must know that you're human too. Share a little about your personal life – but not too much. Just enough to show that you understand what it's like to have responsibilities outside of work. If they never hear you talk about your family or commitments, they'll assume you don't care about theirs.

When someone comes to you with news – like buying a home or expecting a child – that's not a distraction. That's data. That's your opportunity to show care, to build loyalty. Celebrate with them. Help them. Fill out their employment verification paperwork quickly. These moments build lifelong loyalty.

A happy employee tells others. That helps with recruiting. They work harder. That builds culture. It's a cycle, and it starts with you.

6. The Cost of Disconnection
If instead, you dismiss that same employee, delay their paperwork, or show indifference, they'll walk away feeling unvalued. They'll vent to their family and friends. You'll lose their loyalty and possibly the next great hire they might have referred. And when that urgent job comes in, they won't lift a finger to help you.

Good people won't want to work for a leader who doesn't care. Worse, you'll end up with employees just like that; disconnected, bitter, and uncommitted.

7. Know Your Team (Within Limits)
You need to know, within respectful boundaries, your team's life goals, struggles, and values. Why?

- If a key employee is planning to move next year, you can train a replacement now instead of panicking later.

- If someone is underperforming, you'll know whether it's a skill issue, a personal issue, or a motivation issue.
- When they book vacations or make major life decisions, they'll do so with the company in mind because you showed you care.

Proactive leaders prevent problems. Disconnected leaders react too late.

8. Performance Reviews with Purpose

When reviewing performance, be human. Ask first: "Is everything okay?" Remind them of their goals – the house, the vacation, the new car. Help them connect effort at work with the life they want outside of work. That's how you motivate people. When they slip, you can remind them of their dream, not as a threat but as encouragement. They will appreciate that you are looking out for them from a human perspective first, and a business perspective second.

9. Protect the Culture

Weed the weeds and grow the flowers. Toxic employees destroy culture like cancer. But don't let your ego trigger premature decisions. If a difficult employee is valuable, work to coach them first. Only let them go when you've done all you can. And when you do let someone go, do it with dignity. You never know, they might become your future customer or your customer's employee.

10. Keep Politics, Religion, and Identity Out of the Workplace

The workplace is for work. Avoid displaying political symbols, religious icons, or making culturally charged jokes or generalizations. Keep the workplace neutral, inclusive, and focused on team performance and mutual respect. If someone is from your home country (overseas) or of same ethnicity, treat them the same as others. If the common language is English, then everyone should communicate in English.

11. Protect People from Themselves

Sometimes, employees take on more than they can handle. It's your job to step in, not to let them fail. Protect them from burnout. Help them succeed because when they succeed, you succeed.

For example, people get excited when we win a big new project and everyone wants to be involved. Sometimes someone comes to me and says, "I can take on this project. I'll work late and come in on the weekend to get it done." But because I know a little about their personal lives, I say, "Are you sure that's a good idea? You just had a child four weeks ago. How will you manage a new project with all your other projects and new child at home? Perhaps it might be a better idea for you to work on your existing projects and take care of your family. When things are more stable you can take on another project. I really want you to grow, but I also want to protect you and your family."

12. Lead by Example: Energy, Simplicity, and Organization

- **KISS**: Keep it simple, stupid. Be nimble.
  Small manufacturers don't need complexity.
  Complexity costs money, simplicity saves money.
- **Walk the Shop Floor**: Know your business and know your team.
- **Clean Office = Clear Mind**: Your workspace reflects your thinking. Keep it tidy.
- **Energy is Contagious**: If you walk around miserable and angry, everyone feels it. If you radiate energy and motivation, so will they.

13. Communicate with Clarity

Update customers before they ask. Never say you're too busy for a "small customer." Both small and large customers keep you afloat. Never lie to customers, suppliers, or your team. Lies break trust. Communicate in whatever ways work: text, phone, email, video. Stay closely connected.

14. Use Process Thinking, Not Blame Thinking

If something isn't working, don't blame people. Blame the process. Find out what part of the process created the problem. Examine the method. Do they have the right tools? The right training? Is the system supporting the people who do the work? Blame the process, not the people. For example, if an operator keeps making the same mistake, don't jump to the conclusion that the operator is at fault. Investigate first. It could be the machine or the fixture. These would need to be mistake-proofed to eliminate future mistakes.

15. Invest in the Company First

Don't milk the business dry and expect it to thrive. Reinvest profits in machines, in employees, in training. The luxury car and vacation home can come later, when your team is thriving and your business is stable.

Many new businesses fail because the second it generates profit, the owner goes out and leases an expensive new car and buys things that don't generate money. The owner should focus on what generates profit and not act as a consumer and consume the company. Soon, the owner discovers that they need to buy a new machine or have to fix the air conditioning system or they get a large tax bill. They cannot cover those expenses because all the cash is drained for personal use. So, they end up taking a loan, perhaps on top of other loans, until the business sinks into debt. The owner must not put themselves and the company in that position.

16. Handle Conflict with Emotional Maturity

If a customer is angry, pause before responding. Don't let your ego speak. Investigate first. Then, tell or show the customer what you found. Apologize if needed. Offer a recovery plan. Never burn bridges with customers, employees, or suppliers. You never know who will become who tomorrow.

17. Be a Servant Leader

As your business grows, walk the floor. Check in with your team. You and your managers must treat employees as internal customers, with the same respect and urgency you give external customers. Leadership doesn't scale unless humility scales with it.

As you are walking the office and shop floor, are you building trust? Are you making employees feel less intimidated? If so, it creates a bridge where employees will come forward to you with problems. The fact that you listened and cared goes a long way. Problems in the office and shop floor create opportunities to develop and improve the leadership team. And, importantly, it results in a "make problems visible" culture. You never want a "hide the problems" culture.

18. Always Be a Student

You will never have it all figured out. Take notes. Keep a journal. Write things down. It shows care and helps you process what is happening. Reflect on your actions daily. Stay humble. Stay generous. Be grateful for those who helped you succeed.

I often tell the team, "You know what, I learned something new from you today." It's a humble gesture to say that you learned from them It shows you   don't

Know everything and that you can learn. The result is that they open up to you when you try to teach them. It also improves communication.

19. Stay Alert – The Market Won't Wait for You
A leader must stay vigilant. Detect risk early. Sense shifts in the environment, changes in customer demand, supply chain delays, payment issues, employee dynamics, and adjust quickly. Complacency is risk, delay is danger. If you ignore what's changing, it might be too late when it finally hits. Don't let your team and business suffer because you looked the other way.

20. Cash Flow is King
Yes, profit matters. But cash flow matters more. It's the blood of your business. You can be profitable on paper and still go broke if you're not collecting. Prioritize collections. Stay on top of invoices. Build a system where money flows back in with discipline and urgency.

21. Every Failure is a Lesson – If You're Paying Attention
Stressful situations, breakdowns, and mistakes are your greatest teachers. Whether you're a leader or an employee, your attitude toward failure determines whether you grow or regress. The lesson is always there. Whether you see it or not, that's up to you.

22. Right People, In the Right Jobs
A business only wins when the right people are in the

right jobs. The right people follow the company's values even when no one is looking. The right person means they fit the job skills and have the intelligence and motivation to do the job well. If someone is missing one of these, we can't wait forever for them to develop. The longer it takes, the more it slows the whole company down.

Leadership expert John C. Maxwell highlights some truths that every leader must understand:

- Wrong person in the wrong place = **Regression**
- Wrong person in the right place = **Frustration**
- Right person in the wrong place = **Confusion**
- Right person in the right place = **Progress**
- The right people in the right places = **Multiplication**

Your job as a leader is to constantly assess employees' strengths and align them with the jobs that suit them best – but not forever. Most employees have a desire to develop and grow in their current job and want to learn new jobs. Know their aspirations. Inspire them to seek new roles. Place people where they can succeed and where the company can succeed with them, but don't pigeon-hole anyone. They will resent you for doing that. Help employees develop and grow so that they can become more valuable contributors. And you will have much less employee turnover.

23. Develop Talent – Use Structured Feedback

Too often, feedback that managers give to employees is unstructured, not specific, not actionable, late, or not given at all. Employees want to know, and deserve to know, how they are doing.

Each manager should create a simple spreadsheet to make note of what each employee does well (could be many items) and what needs improvement (should be few so as not to overwhelm them). Record this information daily. It does not have to be for every employee every day. It could be one or two employees today, a different employee tomorrow, etc. Record the information in a few words or short sentences and input quickly, in 30 seconds or a minute or two. Do it daily. Then, use the information as part of periodic performance appraisals. This way you will not have to recall things that happened months ago.

Lynn Welding Lynn Welding Co., Inc.	QMSF-1108 Employee Performance Statement	Rev. 3.2
	Effective Date: 07/06/2022	Page 1 of 1
Not controlled in hard copy	Document available electronically QMSF-1108	

Employee Information

Employee Name:		Employee ID:	
Title:		Department:	
Hired Since:		Supervisor:	

Performance Evaluation

Performance Factors	Avg. to Date	2024 Avg.	H1 Avg.	Jan	Feb	March	April	May	June	Trend	H2 Avg.	July	Aug	Sept	Oct	Nov	Dec	Trend
Quality	#DIV/0!		####							####	####							####
Reliablity	#DIV/0!		####							####	####							####
Output	#DIV/0!		####							####	####							####
Teamwork / Cooperativeness	#DIV/0!		####							####	####							####
Cleaniness / Safety	#DIV/0!		####							####	####							####
Adaptability	#DIV/0!		####							####	####							####
Overall Average	#DIV/0!	####	####	####	###	####	####	####	###	####	####	####	####	####	####	####	####	####

Definitions for each rating 1-5	1 = Improvement Req'd 2 = Development Req'd 3 = Meets Expecations 4 = Exceeds Expctations 5 = Far Exceeding

Adaptability = Follows company policy/ procedures, support new rules & changes   Reliablity = Attendance & break time habits

Teamwork / Cooperativeness = Working with others, professional, friendliness   Quality = Quality of work & accuracy

Cleaniness / Safety = Work area cleanliness, housekeeping, safety PPE...etc   Output = Performans work in a timely, professional manner & efficiency

24. Don't Waste Interns – Build the Next Generation

Hiring an intern is a huge responsibility. You're shaping how the next generation sees the world of work. Don't hire them just to figure it out later. Have a plan for them. Equip them. Train them. Challenge them. Don't let them sit bored, scrolling social media, or pushing paper in a corner. Interns are investments. Many future leaders started that way, but only if someone believed in them from the start. An intern's bad experience is a bad reflection on you and the company. It will be harder to hire interns in the future.

25. Hire for Values – Train for Skills

When hiring, don't just look for technical skills or résumé highlights. That's only the surface. The real foundation is the prospective employee's values.

- You can teach someone how to run a machine, but you can't teach someone how to be honest.
- You can train someone to use software, but you can't train someone to take ownership.

If a person doesn't have integrity, self-respect, or accountability baked into who they are, no amount of training will fix it. So be intentional in your interviews. Ask about teamwork, past decisions, how they handled mistakes or conflict, and if they owned the problems. Look for signs of character because that's what your company will live or die on.

26. Stay Calm – That's When You Lead Best

The calmer you are the clearer you think. Don't let stress cloud your judgment. Decisions made in panic often create bigger problems than the ones you're trying to solve. Take a breath, as long as you need, to regain your emotional footing. Then act.

27. Leadership is Like Flying a Plane – Even Small Changes Matter

When you are a leader, you're the pilot of the plane. A small shift in direction early on can send the whole team miles off course. If you are unclear, inconsistent, or making decisions reactively, you could be steering the business away from its goals without even knowing it. That's why you must pause, assess, and think deeply before making key decisions. Don't lead based on your mood. Don't shoot from the hip. Because while the team is busy working, you're the one holding the compass.

28. Avoid the Firefighting Trap – Build the Right Team

Airbnb's founder once said, "When you don't have the right team, you end up doing everyone else's jobs." That's the cycle: wrong hires → firefighting mode → burnout → business suffers. Don't settle. If you are short-staffed, don't lower your hiring standards just to fill a seat. The wrong hire today creates more chaos tomorrow. Do what's right, not what's easy.

29. Organization is Leadership – Eliminate Clutter

A cluttered inbox can cost you a customer. A messy desk can cost you focus. Disorganization hides opportunity. It sends the wrong message to your team. From your email inbox to your shop floor, keep things clear, simple, and clean. You might not see a direct return on investment from repainting your walls or organizing your shelves, but you'll feel it in customer trust, employee pride, and long-term loyalty. People want to be part of something they can be proud of.

30. Your Leadership Impacts Mental Health – Use That Power Wisely

As a leader, the way you treat your employees can influence their stress levels, emotional state, and overall well-being. You can easily give employees anxiety. You need to be aware of that. A kind word, a fair decision, a thoughtful conversation. These things matter. Your actions can build people up or tear them down. Choose to build.

31. How You Treat Young Workers Shapes Their View of Work

If you run a restaurant, gas station, or a shop and hire teenagers for summer help, remember this: You are shaping how they see the working world. If you yell, scare, or ignore them, they'll grow up thinking work is something to fear or avoid. But if you teach, encourage, and guide, you plant seeds of confidence and resilience. That type of leadership lasts for decades. And you will be known and remembered as the rare leader who cares.

32. You Don't Have to Win Every Argument

Sometimes it's okay to lose a conversation with a customer or vendor for the sake of the bigger picture. You don't need to prove you're right every time. Focus on long-term trust, not short-term ego. Sometimes, letting the other person think they have outsmarted you can serve a larger strategy you are pursuing. That's leadership through maturity.

33. Take Care of Yourself – It's Not Selfish, It's Necessary

You can't run a business, lead a team, or take care of your family if you're running yourself into the ground. How many times have we heard: "He worked too hard, had a heart attack, and now the business is gone"? Behind every exhausted leader is a fragile system waiting to fall. Employees lose jobs. Families suffer. Customers walk away. It's your job to stay healthy, present, and stable because too many people are counting on you.

34. Your Words Echo Farther Than You Think
In leadership, your words aren't just heard, they're magnified. Imagine you're reviewing jobs and say: "Skip this one, I don't care about it." Even if you didn't mean it that way, your team might think the job doesn't matter and they'll treat it like it doesn't. That affects quality, customer satisfaction, and company culture.

Instead, say: "We've done this before. I trust the team to handle it like always. Let's focus on the new ones." Same direction, but a different tone and better outcome. Your language sets the tone for the company, so make it count.

35. Build Your Culture on Shared Values
For me and my colleagues, these are the values that matter deeply. They should matter for you as well.

- **Hardworking**: Nothing is worse than carrying the load while others slack off. We surround ourselves with people who give 100 percent.
- **Growth-Oriented**: We face difficulty head-on. We're not afraid of complex challenges. We thrive in them.
- **Quality-Driven**: We do our best work, every time. Not because we have to, but because we care.

- **Honest & Respectful:** No liars. No disrespect. Period.
- **Safe & Clean:** We protect each other and keep our space clean because health and safety are non-negotiable.
- **Family-Focused:** If we don't take care of our families, we can't take care of business. Balance matters.

These values aren't just posters on the wall. They are our daily focus. They're the expectations for anyone who walks through our doors.

36. Instill Confidence in Employees

Employees come from varied backgrounds and work experiences. They may have worked in companies where managers denigrated them personally or their work. They may have lost confidence or never had much confidence. It is the leader's job to instill confidence in employees and hope for better.

Or, some employees may be hypersensitive to feedback because of certain life or work experiences. You cannot assume every employee will handle feedback well. It is better to assume the opposite. Put in the effort to understand each employee better so that you can provide feedback in ways that will be accepted and acted upon. This too will help build employees' confidence.

37. Build a Strong Team

If you are a small business owner working until 10 p.m. at night, have a vacation home, a boat, but no freedom, that's not good. True wealth is to have balance and able to have freedom, and that doesn't happen without building a strong team to support you.

38. Don't be Greedy

Don't lie and play "poor" all the time, people know you have money especially if the business is doing well. Don't be greedy. Pay your team fairly and because that will build loyalty, ownership, mutual respect, and employee retention.

39. When You Let an Employee Go, Stand by the Decision

Firing someone is never easy – and it shouldn't be. It usually follows weeks or months of discussion, coaching, and giving the employees opportunities to improve. And yet, after termination, it is common to second-guess yourself especially if the person comes back asking for another chance. But here's the truth: If you gave them multiple opportunities to improve and they still didn't follow through, your decision was made for the right reasons.

Remind yourself why you took that step. Recall the behaviors, performance, or attitude that led you to terminate their employment. Don't let guilt talk you into reversing a decision that protects your standards, your team, and your company. Letting someone go isn't about punishment, it's about alignment. And if that person wasn't aligned, bringing them back only restarts the same cycle. When terminating people's job, be kind, be fair, be firm, and be confident in your decision.

The best leaders don't just build teams. They shape the company's culture with clear intention. And culture starts with who you let in and who you're willing to let go. You must protect what you are building so that everyone can flourish. And it is important that you train your team on all these points.

40. Help Your Team Get Back to Reality

Employees often see attractive looking job postings or hear about bigger wages or salaries on social media platforms. They think, "Wow, I should be paid that." They might then blame the company for what they think is low pay. They might become upset and angrily confront you. Don't act the same way and start to think, "This person is crazy. Get out."

Instead, sit down with them and ask how they came up with this information. "What led you to think that you can go from 20 dollars an hour to 45 dollars an hour? Where is this job positing?" Look at the job posting with them. Point out that they will need to work longer hours or must have a master's degree or special professional certifications which they do not have.

Explain how and why this amount of pay does not match their qualification, how and why it is a completely different skills set. If they want to try to get that job, you can't stop them. But what you can do is help them face reality and explain that you are paying them fairly for their qualifications.

If they want higher pay, then they need to gain additional skills in the company and perhaps additional education outside the company. You might be able to help with both. When the employee understands reality and you treat their concern with respect, it builds trust and respect.

41. Be Honest
Take audits, which most leaders view as a burden, as learning and improvement opportunities. The auditor is a human coming to do their job to help you improve. Most of the time, the auditor does not know you or your company. They are just trying to do their job. So be honest and own the problems they find. Work with them and they will work with you.

If you try to hide things, lie and act smart, you will eventually get caught and they will make a note that you are not to be trusted. Things will be bad for you, your team, and the company.

42. Make the Workplace Safe
People need to feel safe telling the truth, even when

they make mistakes. If the team is scared, they will hide problems, and small problems will grow into bigger problems. If the team trusts each other, problems get fixed fast without the negativity and lasting effect of blaming people. Thank employees for telling the truth and perhaps give them a small bonus to emphasize the importance of speaking up, and that it is always safe to do so.

43. Remember Your Purpose

A business needs a purpose; something worth fighting for, and not just money. Have a purpose that makes people feel proud to show up every day. When the purpose is real, people stick around and give you their best efforts. For example, we always say, "We want to be the best aerospace welding company in America. It will take some time, but we will get there."

• • • • • •

In a small business, leadership is personal. It's close. Every decision you make ripples across your team, your customers, and your future. Being a small business leader is not just about running a company. It requires constantly sensing, adjusting, and guiding your team through change, pressure, and growth. It is about building people while building the business. Lead with wisdom, build trust, strategic clarity, and create a winning culture. This is what real leadership looks like: No ego. No excuses. Just purpose, people, and progress. Let this be your daily compass.

You must train and shape your future leaders in all the areas above so that you can gain more freedom and continue to move forward and thrive.

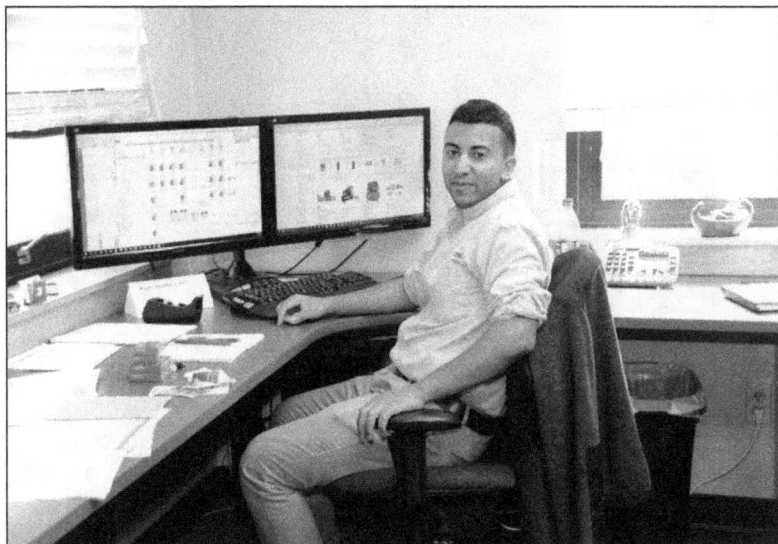

Doing engineering work, circa 2017

Darius Kania and Ibrahim at the new acquisition, Associated Spot Welders. The company was closed the first week of October 2024 to rapidly do a complete renovation of the facility.

3

Passion, Persistence, Humility, and Heart

Successful businesses are built on more than just strategy and systems. It's also built on the character of the leaders. Behind a great team, a strong culture, and business results are leaders, managers, supervisors, and workers who show up every day with a passion for the work, persistence through challenges, humility to keep learning from any source, and the heart to lead with care and good judgment. These are the foundation of leadership and business growth. Here's what they mean, and why they matter.

Heart, Habits, and Building a Workplace That Works

Every successful business has people, machines, and systems, but the secrets for success are much harder to see. The secrets – passion, persistence, humility, and heart – sound simple, but putting them into practice every day, by all members of the management team, is difficult.

Passion means loving what you do so much that you can't wait to start your day. It's the motivation, the fire that burns inside that drives you forward to produce, bit by bit, the desired human, company, and customer outcomes. **Persistence** is staying the course, especially when setbacks occur. It means being adaptable and meeting with your team to make changes in a timely manner. Never procrastinate, move thoughtfully and quickly. Consistency wins over time. It is better to be someone who won't quit rather than being smartest person in the room.

Humility can be the toughest of all because it is hard to keep one's ego in check, hard to always respect every employee – even the difficult ones – and keep learning. If you become arrogant, you will stop learning and make damaging mistakes. **Heart** defines *why* you do it. The company must generate profit, but people's daily work is how profit is generated. It's remembering that behind every job there is a human being; a family and a life story that matters. So, remember:

Passion keeps you moving.
Persistence keeps you going.
Humility keeps you learning.
Heart keeps you human.

This passage is inspired by the pioneering Egyptian heart surgeon Sir Magdi Yacoub.

One-on-One Meetings: Building Trust, Retaining Talent

For the past 10 years, I've made it a point to do one-on-one satisfaction meetings with my team. As the business grows and I prepare to hand off daily operations to our future operations manager, I am continuing the habit of personally meeting with employees who request it and encouraging my leadership team to do the same. It's a powerful method for improving employee retention. And it complements our anonymous employee surveys and year-round digital feedback forms.

In these meetings, I focus not just on the job, but on the person. What are their goals? Do they feel they are fairly compensated? Do they feel respected by their direct supervisor? Is anything happening in their personal life that's affecting their performance? We shake hands, we talk honestly. If someone asks for a raise, but the data shows underperformance, I say: "Let's get you back on your feet. I want you to succeed. We have the money, but it has to be earned." And people appreciate that style of communication – truthful, direct, and human.

Confrontation Isn't Fun – But Avoiding It Is Worse

A lot of managers hate confrontation. That's a natural human response, but an unnatural response for leaders. Being a leader means gaining the necessary productive skills for handling conflicts and confrontation. If you avoid conflict, then you will never gain the skill that every leader must have. Engage when necessary and do so in a thoughtful and timely manner. If you don't, who will? So, face it on your terms, but with structure and compassion, before the problem blows up on you. The better you handle these situations, the more you will be trusted and respected.

The same goes for performance reviews. In many companies, managers rush through the performance appraisal forms with no data or clear recollection of why someone is doing well or not. When employees expect a raise and don't get it, managers often panic and make something up. That damages trust and culture. That's why I ask managers to document weekly feedback. Just a line or two of text in a spreadsheet is all that is needed.

Twice a year, we review the data with each employee. If they are doing well, we praise them and identify one or two things they can improve upon. We say, "Remember that job you crushed last quarter? I want to see more of that. Let's get you that raise so that you can buy that BMW you've been dreaming about." When performance is down, we use real examples and support the person's development. Never attack them with a barrage of negative feedback. We point out specific problems and say encouraging things, "I believe in you. I know you can perform better. You've done it in the past. It's a challenge that you can handle."

Sometimes I just say it like this: "Listen, this is very stressful for me. It is no fun to sit down and have this tough conversation. I hate it and it keeps me up at night thinking about how to discuss this. But I know we have to have this conversation one way or another, so let's help each other get it done for you and me and for the company. We can't just ignore it; we have to talk."

Performance Tools That Work: The Red/Green Card System

In our manual Fusion Welding department, we are testing a Red/Green Card system that's become one of our best motivational tools. Each welder can earn up to 15 green cards a week, 3 per day, which equates to a $150 weekly bonus (up to $1,800 per quarter). It creates healthy competition, increases retention, and rewards based on merit. Mistakes earn red cards, and exceptional work earns gold cards worth $100. Since implementing it, our welding department has consistently been our top performer and that's no coincidence. People perform better when ownership is clear, rewards are fair, and feedback is real.

Walking the Floor: More Than Just "Checking In"

For a decade, I walked the floor every single morning Now, with a more challenging schedule, I do it two to three times a week while the managers perform the daily walkthroughs. But daily walkthroughs aren't just to say hello. There's deep psychological value in showing up. When leaders walk the floor consistently, employees feel seen. They want to show you what they're working on and their new ideas. They want to know that you notice. If you're absent for weeks and suddenly show up, people start to get nervous. They hide problems and change their behavior. You then lose visibility. That's how blind spots form. And blind spots lead to bad decisions.

So, I stop by different people. A quick hello here. A follow-up there. I say congratulations for the newborn or a birthday. A quick handshake for a passed test. Walking the floor is also an opportunity to show appreciation and say, "thank you" and provide encouragement whether someone is going well or not. People notice when you show up and take an interest in them, their work, and their team – especially when they know how busy you are. And when they say, "Thanks for making time," I always reply: "This is my job. I'm never too busy for you. I'm here to serve."

Helping Underperformers: Support Before Discipline

When someone is underperforming, you can't start by attacking them. You start with care: "How are things? Is there anything major going on outside of work?" If the answer is no, you move forward: "That's good to hear. I've been noticing some changes in your performance, and I want to talk about how we can get you back on track." No threats. No intimidation. Just honest, fact-based conversation. If the problems continue, follow up: "We talked about this two weeks ago. We agreed on a plan. What's holding you back?" Eventually, if improvement doesn't come, then discipline may follow. But don't give up too quickly, especially on people who've been great in the past.

Some employees just need help getting back on track. That's your job as a leader. If the issue is misalignment, not performance, have the courage to say: "I understand you disagree with this direction. But this change is for the good of the company. Let's find common ground. I can't make exceptions for individuals, but I want to help you adapt before we decide this isn't the right fit." Don't jump to "do it or go." Try everything before getting to that point.

Make the Workplace a Place You'd Be Proud to Visit

A clean, well-organized workplace matters, not just for employees but for customers too. You want customers to walk in and say "Wow!" You want your employees to be proud to say, "I work here!" But too often, owners live in beautiful homes and drive nice cars, while the shop is hot, dirty, has flickering lights, leaking pipes, and is smelly. And yet we spend more of our lives at the workplace than at home.

So, invest in the company and the people. Install proper lighting and air conditioning. Fix the bathrooms. Use the same soap and amenities that you would use at home. Build a nice kitchen and eating area. Buy a refrigerator and a good coffee machine. You're not just building a business. You're building a place where people live a third of their lives. Make it clean. Make it inspiring. Make it worthy of your team and yourself.

I often hear from the leaders of other companies that they spend half their day at work. Half your day is half your life, so, make it fun for yourself. You work to have a good life and grow, so enjoy the journey. You don't have to suffer because suffering is avoidable.

4

Guidance for Employees

For Leaders: Leading a small business involves lots of daily interaction with employees. Like a sports coach, the leader's job is to "coach up" employees to higher levels of performance. So that means a lot of communication to explain what is expected and help them overcome their barriers. Here are my tips to help guide your interactions with employees. Or, better yet, share these tips with your employees.

For Employees: In life and work, we all go through seasons – highs, lows, changes, and challenges. But how we handle those moments says everything about our mindset, our maturity, and our commitment to work and the life we want to build. Here's some perspective to keep you steady, strong, and growing no matter what life throws your way.

1. Life Lessons for Employees in a Small Business

a) The Wisdom of Silence
- Silence in need = **Dignity**
- Silence in provocation = **Nobility**
- Silence in success = **Confidence**
- Silence in failure = **Strength**
- Silence in hardship = **Patience**

Speak when your words add value. Otherwise, let your actions speak louder.

b) Focus on Growth, Not on Others

Don't compare yourself to lazy coworkers. Compare yourself to those moving up. Focus on *your* growth. Compete with *yourself*, not others.

c) Success is Balance

- Winning at work but failing at home = **Failure**
- Winning at home but failing at work = **Failure**
- Succeeding at both = **True Success**

Find your balance. Adjust constantly. Your work and family are both part of your success story.

d) Show Gratitude – It's a Lost Art

If you get a raise or bonus, say thank you. Show appreciation. Acknowledge effort. And don't obsess over chasing money — that leads to blindness. Focus instead on mastery. Skills. Results. The money follows those who earn it.

e) Don't Burn Bridges

Sometimes things do not go as you would like. If the job or the company is not a good fit for you, then leave with grace. Keep in mind that the boss or co-worker that you don't like today could become your client or your new manager tomorrow. Always exit with dignity.

f) Control Your Emotions

You can't see your reflection in boiling water. And you can't see the truth when you're angry. Never make a decision in anger because it will likely be the wrong decision. Don't threaten; it's not professional.

g) Accept and Act Upon Feedback

Feedback from a boss can be difficult to take especially if one has had life or work experiences where feedback was given thoughtlessly or in untimely ways. People get very sensitive when that happens. If needed, talk to your boss about how or when you prefer to receive feedback. This will help you grow and improve and become a more valuable employee.

2. Daily Practices That Build Great Careers

For employees at any level, here's what separates the good from the great:

- Set daily, weekly, and monthly goals.
- Write things down, always, so you don't forget.
- Follow up, internally and externally.
- Say: "Just to make sure I understand…" (then repeat what they said).
- Be flexible. Wear different hats.
- Don't ask for more if you haven't mastered the minimum.
- Don't leave tasks 90 percent done. Finish what you start.
- When overwhelmed, pause and plan, then commit.

- Be logical. Know your market value
- Save money always. $1 or $500 a week. Save something

3. Don't Fear the Skilled – Fear the Lazy
When a new employee arrives, some employees feel threatened. Don't be. Skilled people don't harm teams, they help them. It's the lazy, the insecure, the dishonest who create toxicity. Strong people build. Weak people scheme. Love yourself, yes, but don't harm others just to get ahead. If you're thirsty enough, you'll dig a well. In other words: if you want something, you'll find a productive way of getting it.

4. What Kind of Employee Are You?
There are three types of employees:

- **Low Level of Drive and No Vision**
  Starts strong, gets lazy, focuses on lifestyle, loses job, starts over.
- **Medium Drive But Gets Comfortable**
  Rises quickly, gets complacent, performance drops, resets again.
- **High Drive: Long-Term Growth**
  Always learning. Always growing. Always improving. These are the ones who go the distance. These are tomorrow's leaders.

Which one are you?

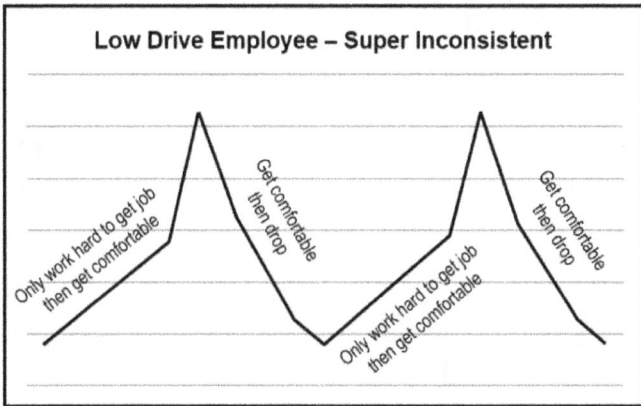

Low Drive Employee – Super Inconsistent

Only work hard to get job then get comfortable

Get comfortable then drop

Only work hard to get job then get comfortable

Get comfortable then drop

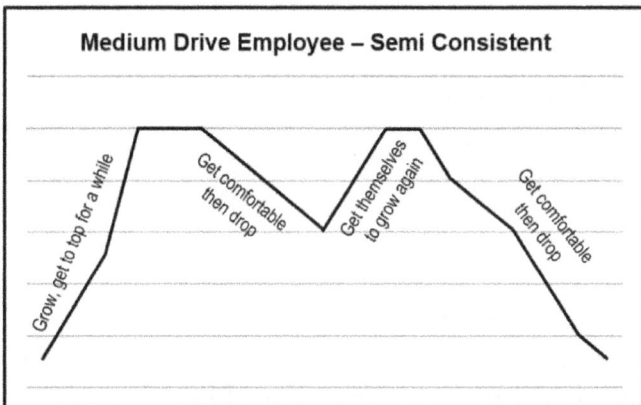

Medium Drive Employee – Semi Consistent

Grow, get to top for a while

Get comfortable then drop

Get themselves to grow again

Get comfortable then drop

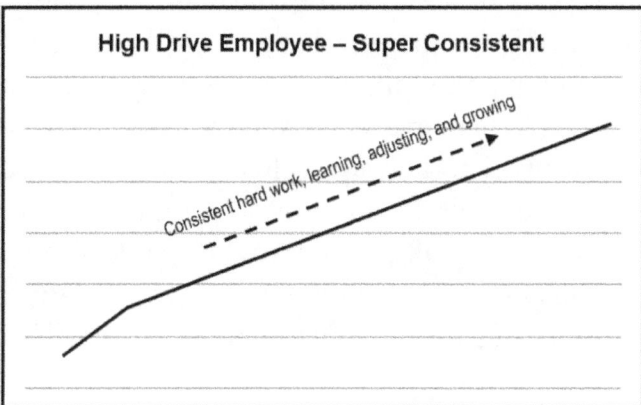

High Drive Employee – Super Consistent

Consistent hard work, learning, adjusting, and growing

5. Stay Motivated

Work every week like it's your first. Stay hungry. The moment you feel too comfortable, you're moving backward. Your future is in your hands. Show up, care deeply, and never stop learning and trying out new ideas. A small business is a place where growth, loyalty, and legacy can be built – but only if everyone, from the top down, does the hard work of showing up with clarity, integrity, and care.

Whether you're a leader or an employee, this is what matters:

- Stay calm
- Stay focused
- Stay learning
- And most of all, stay human

6. Own Your Work

Take ownership for your work. Always think about the person after you in the process. Don't inconvenience the next person because the process was completed incorrectly. If people send their work to the next person and have the mindset, "It's not my job, let them deal with it," then everyone suffers. Think about the person after you and always deliver 100 percent defect-free work. Also, it is not just important to do your work, but it is equally important to think about how you can improve the work you or your team does. Make continuous improvement part of your daily work.

7. Life Will Test You – Don't Quit

Everyone will face major life changes at some point; becoming a parent, losing someone you love, or dealing with health issues. These things change who you are. That's the human experience. When those moments come, be honest with your employer. Talk to them. Don't isolate yourself or suffer in silence.

At the same time, be reasonable and fair. For example, if you have a sick child and spend six months underperforming (which is understandable), don't expect the same performance bonus you received when you were at your peak. No one's punishing you, it's just the reality of your situation and of performance-based pay systems.

Own your journey. Don't blame others. Work with your team to find a path forward. You'll earn respect from others.

8. Hard Work Is the Real Path to Peace of Mind

There are no shortcuts or secrets. Just consistent, focused effort. Those who work hard during the day sleep well at night. There is peace of mind in knowing you gave your best. Some people say they "just want to rest." But here's the truth: if you really want rest, work hard. Not working is what builds anxiety, overthinking, regret, and frustration. Work clears the mind. Work isn't punishment. It is purpose.

Ask yourself this: "Why doesn't your heart take a break?" Your heart beats 24/7/365. It never rests. The moment it does, life ends. The same goes for your work ethic. When it stops, your momentum, your growth, and your opportunities end too. Too much comfort leads to decline. Too much rest leads to weakness. Hard work gives you purpose. It gives you life.

9. Don't Get Comfortable – Stay Driven

We all face obstacles. We all go through change. But the people who grow are the ones who win long-term. They keep showing up, even when it's hard. They understand the expectations of the managers: put in good effort, improve steadily, and be consistent. Keep moving forward. It can be tough at times, but most people can do it. Comfort is the enemy of progress. The minute you think you have "arrived," you start moving backward.

10. Have Self-Reality

You'll meet plenty of people who manage their money poorly and then turn around and say, "I don't get paid enough." The truth is, it's not always about how much you make, it's about how you manage it. Save more, stop complaining, and don't assume others are doing better just because they drive a nice car or own a big house. They might actually make less money than you do, but they are smarter about how they handle their finances. Be real with yourself. Have self-reality

11. Do It with the Right Mindset

If you're given a task you don't like, or a project you hate, you've got two choices. You can do it with a smile, see it as a new challenge, and treat it like a chance to learn something new. When you think that way, you will do well. You'll prove you can handle tough situations, and you'll grow.

Or you can complain. You can make excuses about why it can't be done instead of figuring out how to make it happen. That mindset will make you fail, expose your weaknesses, and keep you moving backward. The choice is always yours.

12. Get to Work On Time

Coming to work on time is important. If you are always late by even 5 minutes, you're still late. Sooner or later you'll have an uncomfortable conversation with your boss. Plan your day so that you arrive 15 minutes early so that even if you hit traffic or other delay, you still arrive on time. If you arrive early, you get to settle in and prepare to start day without rushing. This is important for managers too because they set not only an example but the tone for the day. Arriving on time, or a little early, is what every employee must do.

13. Stay Neutral and Avoid Drama

You don't have to be best friends with your co-workers or managers. You don't even have to like them, and they don't have to like you. What matters is alignment to get things done. Work together, stay professional, and focus on winning people through respect and consistency, not gossip or cliques.

Avoid talking badly about someone just because you trust another person at work. The moment you have a conflict with that trusted person, everything can flip, and suddenly you're the one who looks bad. Stay neutral. Stay out of drama. Don't waste energy on gossip or petty things that add no value.

Remember, you're there to make a living, to grow, and to provide for your family. Friendships at work can happen naturally over time, but your priority will always be your growth and your family's well-being. Never forget that.

14. Handle Conflict the Right Way

If you have a conflict with someone, especially a manager, deal with it behind closed doors. Always talk it out directly and professionally. Walking around complaining to your co-workers doesn't make things better, it just spreads negativity. When you do that, you're not just speaking badly about a person, you're speaking badly about the company. And that never ends well.

No one can fix your situation but you. Face it, figure out how to align, and if a new role or situation doesn't fit, go speak with HR or leadership. They're the ones who can actually help you. Don't waste time venting to the wrong people.

And if things still don't work out, leave the company respectfully. The world is small and reputations travel. When your name comes up, you want people to say, "They were great. It was just a misalignment with the company," not "They were a pain, and we're glad they're gone." The choice is always yours.

• • • • • •

Remember, always act like it's your first week on the job. Be humble. Be hungry. Keep learning and building your skills. Don't wait for someone to push you to be better, push yourself. That's how careers are built. That's how people elevate themselves from good to great.

Managers may not say it often or often enough, but they do value their employees. The tips listed above will help you become a valued employee and lead to new opportunities.

Renovating Associated Spot Welders in
October 2024.

5

Customer Focus, Communication, and Culture

In a fast-moving manufacturing environment, production managers are more than task planners they are communicators, coordinators, and culture builders. Success isn't just about moving parts through various departments. It is about how you keep customers informed, how you lead your teams, and how you respond when things go wrong. Here's how we do it and why it matters.

Start with Discipline: Status Updates and Flow

Every new job that enters the shop starts a chain reaction. That's why we follow a tight communication process from the moment we receive a new order:

- Email the sales order acknowledgment (SOA) within 24 hours.
- Send the estimated ship date (ESD) within 24 hours.
- Notify the customer when we start the job.
- Email a shipping notification when the job is complete.

These steps build trust, reduce confusion, and give customers peace of mind. But sending emails isn't enough; accuracy matters. That means:

- Double-checking shipping requirements.
- Confirm fixturing, test coupons, special tooling, and material status.
- Setting realistic due dates. No guesswork, no "we'll figure it out later" thinking.

Clarify Roles: Who Owns What

When jobs touch multiple departments (e.g., Purchasing → Fusion → Resistance), clarity on process ownership is critical. Every cross-functional job must have a clear point of contact. That way, customers don't get bounced around and internal confusion doesn't lead to dropped balls.

Whether it's a high-dollar order, a long lead time, or a multi-step project, we always assign the right program manager or production manager to own customer communication from start to finish.

Master the Art of eMail

Customer communication is a reflection of your professionalism. That's why we have specific standards:

- Attach all files as PDFs (or JPEGs for images)
- Keep attachments under 10-12 MB; use SharePoint or ZIP files if needed
- Acknowledge every customer email, no exceptions
- Always "Reply All" so the team stays in the loop

- Copy the appropriate team (e.g., fusion@, resistance@)
- Use read receipts for important updates or delay notifications
- Maintain clean formatting: 12 point font, proper spacing, and readable images

Read it twice before hitting send. Sloppy customer communication signals sloppy work. And sloppy work drives customers away.

Don't Say "No" – Say It Better

Customers don't want to hear "No." But they respect honesty when it's delivered with effort and care. Let's say a customer needs a rush order back by Friday, but it's impossible due to non-destructive testing (NDT) requirements. Instead of saying, "No, we're short on staff," say, "Thank you for the heads-up. Unfortunately, due to NDT requirements, we won't be able to deliver by Friday afternoon. That process alone takes one business day. We'll do everything we can to complete by Monday morning. We understand the urgency and will keep you informed."

And then, pick up the phone. Follow up with a call. Show you care. Show you're real. That's how you build long-term customer loyalty.

Investigate Before You Respond

When a customer reports a problem, like missing parts,

don't rush to defend.

This is bad: "I was at shipping – I know we sent it."
This is worse: Silence.
This is good: "Thank you for bringing this to our attention. I'll investigate with the team and get back to you by close of business tomorrow."

And again: follow with a call. Customers don't expect perfection. But they do expect you to take ownership and fix what's broken.

When Things Go Wrong – Own It and Improve

If a shipping mistake is confirmed, your reply to the customer matters. Say, "Thank you again for reaching out. We found the missing bag and will ship today on our account. We've added a final part count step after visual inspection to prevent this going forward. We sincerely apologize for the error."

That's how you turn a problem into trust. Don't just patch the mistake. Explain the fix. That's what customers remember.

Know When to Micro-Watch a Job

Some jobs need a closer eye. As a production manager, you must micro-watch the work when it involves:

- A new customer
- A high-risk or high-dollar job
- A rework or late job

- A brand-new job
- A rush or expedited request

This isn't micromanaging, it is smart risk management. It protects your team and your customers from preventable mistakes.

Professionalism Is a Standard – Not a Choice

When production managers show consistency, clarity, and empathy, they set the tone for the rest of the shop. This isn't just entirely about customer service. It is also about building a culture that respects customers and the people in the company who process the job.

- Communicate like a pro
- Document like a pro
- Follow-up like a pro
- Own your process
- Protect the company's reputation
- And above all, treat customers like partners

Because when things get busy, stressful, or unclear, the way we handle customer communication is the difference between losing trust and strengthening it.

The Associated Spot Welding company team.

6
Closing Comments

Every small business story is, at its heart, a human story. It is built one person, one idea, and one risk at a time. When I look back on my journey, from arriving in the United States with a suitcase and a dream to complete a college degree to leading three growing companies, I see the same pattern repeated over and over again: persistence through difficulty, humility in learning, and gratitude for the people who stood beside me. No success happens alone. Every achievement in this book is shared with co-workers, mentors, and family who believed in something better and worked for it every single day.

Running a small manufacturing business demands long hours, deep focus, and the willingness to keep learning even when you think you already know. You will face setbacks that test your patience, moments of doubt that shake your confidence, and challenges that seem unfair. But if you stay grounded and remember why you started, and who you're doing it for, those moments will become the foundation of your leadership style.

There will be some turbulent times – a bubble economy, cancelled contracts, conflict with a supplier or customer, a disgruntled employee, a lawsuit (frivolous or otherwise), etc. Don't let your ego or your emotions control you. Remember that people are relying on you and they should not have to suffer from your stress or your business problem. Their job is to help you and the company continue to grow. So don't lose your sense of humor and keep smiling.

Leadership is not about titles or offices. It's about service to others. It's about taking responsibility for the team, the customer, and the outcome. "Leaders eat last," as the saying goes, but they must also listen first. The real test of leadership is not how loudly you talk when things go well, it's how calmly you act when things go poorly. When the pressure is high, stay steady. When people lose focus, stay centered. When there is conflict, stay kind and stay human. And when the team succeeds, share the credit generously. That's how you build loyalty.

In each chapter of this book, you have seen that growth in business begins with growth in people. Machines and systems are necessary, but it is people who carry the business forward. Invest in them. Teach them. Challenge them. Care for them. A clean shop and an organized office show respect for the work. Listening and fair decision-making show respect for the person. The best leaders understand both. The most effective cultures are the ones where respect flows in every direction – top to bottom, bottom to top, and side to side.

Never lead with ego. Ego clouds judgment. It kills learning and pushes people away. The moment you think you're the smartest person in the room, you stop improving. The best leaders I know ask questions, admit mistakes, enthusiastically invite ideas for improvement. They understand that leadership is not about being right; it's about doing what's right. So, stay open. Keep learning. Seek feedback even when it's uncomfortable. Humility is not weakness; it is strength under control.

Don't let comfort be your downfall. The same habits that built your success can also hold you back if you stop challenging yourself. Keep moving forward. Revisit your systems. Ask if there's a better way. Technology changes, markets change, people change, and so leaders must change too, in step with the times – not behind the times. Complacency is the silent killer of good businesses. Growth happens only when we remain students of our craft and when we develop and guard the culture.

Business is ultimately about people helping other people. Customers trust you because you solve their problems. Employees trust you because you create opportunities. Suppliers trust you because you deal with them fairly. Protect those relationships as if your company's life depends on them, because it does. When you make a promise, deliver. When you make a mistake, own it. When you get ahead, help others rise with you. Success without integrity is failure.

And never forget where you came from. Whether you started with one machine, one employee, or one unpaid internship, remember those early days when every order mattered and every customer phone call was a chance to prove yourself. Gratitude keeps you grounded. It reminds you that even when you lead hundreds of people, you are still part of the same team, working side by side toward something bigger than yourself.

Here are a few things I always try to keep in mind:

- Don't operate your business with ego. Lead with logic, humility, and fairness.

- Don't forget where you came from or the people who helped you get here.

- Don't act emotionally or make big decisions when you're tired, angry, or unsure.

- Don't rush when data is missing or unclear. Think first, act second.

- Keep smiling through good times and bad. Everything passes, and positive attitude is contagious.

- Don't get too comfortable; the moment you do, you can lose it all.

If you follow those principles, you'll not only build a stronger business, but you will also build stronger versions of yourself. Every challenge should refine you; every success should humble you, and every relationship will teach you something new about leadership and life.

My goal with this first edition is to share the foundation, the mindset, the heart, and the practical lessons that have shaped my journey. This book is just the beginning, and I plan to grow it the same way we grow our businesses. In future editions I will share many other things that I have learned that will be useful to leaders, managers, and employees.

As you close this book, I hope you carry one message above all: Small businesses are the backbone of this country, and small business leaders are the heart that keeps it beating. You don't need to be perfect. You just need to care deeply, act decisively, and stay consistent. Build with passion, lead with persistence, learn with humility, and serve with heart. And make work fun so that people enjoy their time at work.

Thank you for taking the time to read my story and my lessons. I wrote this book not only to share what I have learned, but also to honor everyone who works hard, dreams big, and refuses to give up. If this book helps even one small business leader lead better, communicate more clearly, or treat people better, then it has done its job.

Whether you are the owner, a manager, a supervisor, a team leader, or a worker, keep growing. Keep improving. Keep believing in yourself and your team. Success will follow. This is what has worked for me.

Opening a new business, Intelligent Cutting
Solutions, on 9 September 2020.

About the Author

Ibrahim Ibrahim was born in Kafr El Dawar, Beheira, Egypt. He came to the United States in 2010 to pursue a Bachelor of Science in Electromechanical Engineering Technology at Central Connecticut State University (CCSU) in New Britain, Connecticut. He became a U.S. citizen in May 2021.

He started working at Lynn Welding in Newington, Connecticut, a first-tier manufacturer of aerospace welded fabrications, as an intern while pursuing his studies at CCSU. After graduation in 2013, he joined Lynn Welding full-time. He started as a resistance welding process engineer and helped build the technical capabilities and sales growth of the department.

In 2016, Ibrahim was promoted to department manager. In that role he gained the trust of his co-workers throughout the company. At the age of 26, he was promoted to the role of operations manager leading a company of 48 people.

At the age of 28, he partnered with the owner of Lynn Welding to start a new business, Intelligent Cutting

Solutions (ICS, Newington, Connecticut). A few years later, they bought another business, Associated Spot Welders (ASW, City of Industry, California). Combined, the three companies employ 107 people. The companies are known by their numerous large aerospace and commercial customers as an industry leader in quality and customer service.

Presently, Ibrahim is Chief Operating Officer of Lynn Welding. The company has quintupled sales since 2013 and has been recognized in the *Hartford Courant* as a top place to work five years in row. The other two businesses, ICS and ASW, are on a similar growth trajectory.

He has humbly received the following awards:

- CCSU Ebenezer D. Bassett Student Achievement Award, March 2015
- Congressional Recognition, March 2015
- "40 Under 40," *Hartford Business Journal*, August 2018: https://hartfordbusiness.com/honoree/ibrah im-ibrahim/
- Next GEN Industry Award, October 2019, https://www.thomasnet.com/insights/learning-english-at-18-managing-operations-at-26-ibrahim-ibrahim-wins-nextgen-for-industry-award/
- Patriotic Employer Award, "Employer Support of the Guard and Reserve" from the Department of the Secretary of Defense, March 2023

- CCSU Young Alumni Award, June 2023
- Patriotic Employer Award "Employer Support of the Guard and Reserve" from the Department of the Secretary of Defense, April 2024
- Service to organizations
  - American Welding Society D17D Aerospace Welding Committee Board
  - Advisory Board Member, CCSU Department of Manufacturing and Construction Management

Ibrahim is married and has two daughters. They reside in Connecticut. He is known for his perpetual smile.

U.S. Citizenship • My American Dream!